♥ CA

lover boy

letters to my lover

lover boy

letters to my lover

by Courtney Ann

♥ CA

read more of Courtney's work here:

3

❤ CA

First Edition
10 9 8 7 6 5 4 3 2 1

ISBN: 979-8-9934475-2-0

Illustrations: Annie Lou
Cover Design: Courtney Ann

For information, questions, or concerns, please email courtneyann.author@gmail.com.

❤ CA

for your love.
for your kindness.
for sharing patience.
for our forever life.
i love you lover.

❤ CA

contents

♥ CA

on saving

♥ CA

lover boy

lover boy, oh lover boy
how i need you so.
without you there would not be a me,
you absolutely saved this soul.

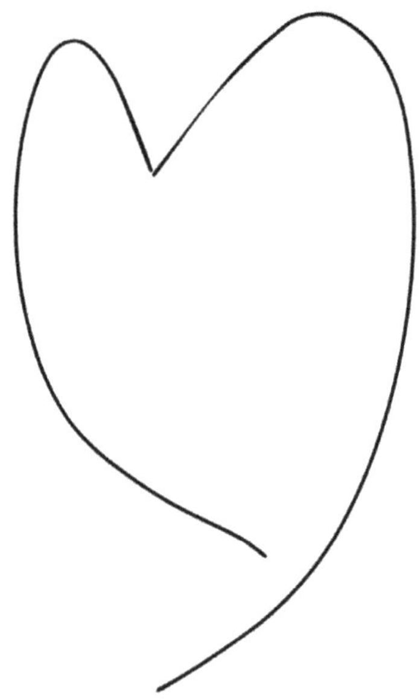

♥ CA

silently screaming

why does your smile make me feel like
i'm burning alive?
why can i feel your sadness
leaking from my eyes?
what's it called,
when i feel what you show outside, inside?
what's it mean when i feel your emotions and mine?
is it referred pain?
is it an overly compassionate mind?
how does it make you feel when i cry?
how can you tell...when you're feeling me or you?
do you get that tightness in your chest?
do you ever think, "will this hurt less?"
what lives in the silence, you ask?
the truth?
trauma makes you emotional, is there anything to do?
you cry and you cry, until all the feels run through.
then wake up the next morning and say,
"you know what? fuck you."

♥ CA

eclipse me, my dark knight

eternal darkness flowing
corpses bleeding growing
leave it alone?
i'll let it roam.
please
show me the way out,
entomb my doubt.

❤ CA

don't let me go

please just a little longer
squeeze me tighter
hold me to your chest
let me feel your breath
i can't regulate right now
my world is crumbling down
you've always been my white night
thank you, for proving that tonight

inside, you will find
a different mind
a different place
a different time
maybe they happened
or it's all a big crock
just make sure you
watch the clock
chiming and clanging
making it's presence known
if you peek inside
the metal comes alive
with every tone
while a happy ending will always follow
the winner at the end
might taste a bit fouler
so follow the Raven if you want to survive
she knows what it's like to be
dead inside.

♥ CA

the voices

get out
get out
get out
get out of my head, my heart, my soul
they never leave
never turn off, no matter how many times i beg
haunting my sanity like ghosts
scratching and clawing
telling me what i know and where to go
silence is what i crave.
just one voice at a time
is that so hard to ask?
unfortunately this disease is lifelong
it's not going to pass.
the cup in my mind is overflowing
my angel, my saving grace
is toxic i'm told
so i've started running
running from the voices, the past, the future, the now
because each day they get louder
i'm not sure how much longer i can tune them out.

❤ CA

i'm fine

i'm fine
i swear, i'm fine
no really, i'm fine
it's loud, but i'm fine
it's bright, but i'm fine
that hurts, but i'm fine
STOP ASKING, i'm fine.

if your concern is so high
in the forefront of your mind
let's send those questions your way
and see what arrives
otherwise **listen**, hear me when i say *i'm fine.*
even if it's not the truth
that means you don't deserve it today.
so thank you, but i'm fine.

💔 CA

why do i automatically cry when a high-energy or intense moment happens? it's like dry eyes to full sob in a second flat. but then i can turn it off...snap...just like that. it feels practiced, but i can't think of a time i've done that. consciously, at least, who knows what my unconscious brain does. only when i'm alone does this happen, though. socially i'd shove those feelings way down, down until i feel it's safe. there's a little flag waving in my mind. i feel like i was told that overly expressing my emotions was wrong. probably because i was so disregulated as a child, they just wanted me to **stop**. i had a hard time controlling these emotions, so maybe that's why i can't help but cry. or maybe my emotional well has finally reached its tipping point and i've blown the top. but seriously, i'm fine. i always feel like this, it'll eventually stop.

❤ CA

ya.

"hey, are you okay?"

"ya, of course. i'm fine."

...just ignore the blood dripping from my eyes.

♥ CA

ghost in the hall

my screams must be silent
there's no way you can't hear me
a ghost wandering the halls
knocking down books and pictures
i know you can see
but when words leave my lips
they don't penetrate
no one *listens* to me.
i'm trying to tell you i'm drowning
that this is too much,
i can't fucking breathe.
please, help me.

❤ CA

cross to bear

i don't trust you
i barely trust me
how can i give you my soul
when she's somewhere lost at sea
i've been burned by water
completely drained of my blood
what does it even mean to love?

❤ CA

spinebreakers

do you know what it's like to feel
sideways while standing up?

try going right
you turn left
take a step back
flat on your ass
three steps forward
well that's a trap

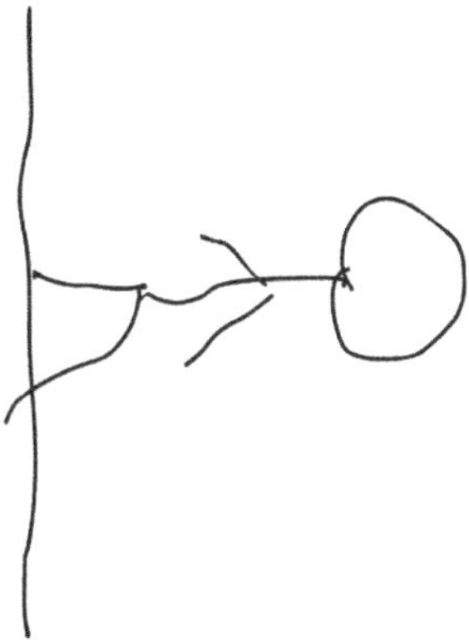

now do it every day
while you work
while you live
while you love
while you play
then pull your head out
of the whirlpool long enough
to enjoy it all and fill your cup,
they say.

if you manage that, well
let a sister know
a spine can only bend so far before breaking
ya know?

you know that feeling
crawling underneath
picking and clawing
at every crack and tear
until you're given no choice
but to break in despair

be yourself—but don't wear that.
be loud and free—but shave please, you look like trash.
be brilliant—just make sure it's perfect, we don't do
second best

there's never a wrong without a right
same way that right goes with wrong
but no matter what you say
it's always *my* right that's wrong
you can't possibly be at fault,
right?

❤ CA

i feel it festering beneath my skin
so deep that it hides the scars within
that was by design, i now know
don't want anything to show
how low your cruelty goes

they say i have nice skin,
but it's just a facade.
underneath it's black and blue
how long will it take
to heal the inside, too?

❤ CA

gaslighting fiends

what would you do?
if everything you believed
sitting core deep
was a lie
a ruse
a manipulation, on repeat.
every day, they're reinforced
with vociferous tweets
never comprehending the damage
that's spreading like weeds.
then one day, it detonates
the truth comes out
and you're supposed to just accept it
no screams, not even a shout.
that's called gaslighting
my fiends and friends.
now here, endure your prize
you'll never trust again
because everyone lies.

❤ CA

car crash through my bedroom door

it's crazy when i think back
on my younger self in this life
i really don't remember seeing a white light
black, maybe blue, some red and purple too
but nothing creamy or bright.
that glow at the end of the tunnel,
just felt waaay out of sight.
the sounds, wow, i feel them now
car crash through my bedroom door.
splinters litter the walls, the ceiling
what the fuck is on the floor?
those fists of fury
banging all night long,
no point in trying to stop it
it's never a fair fight.

i don't do well in loud places,
i run away from spotlights
i wish little annie lou didn't have to live that way
cuz now, she's so *not* fucking alright.

❤ CA

do you ever feel like you're
from a different place?
living in a different time?
the mirror is warped
cracked at the corners
exposing a lost soul—oh how i mourn her.
i swear my knowledge is vast
i just *know* and can't explain that
when i try the words dry up on my tongue
and all you get are little breadcrumbs
is that normal?
does anyone feel the same way?
maybe i'm just on the wrong planet,
caught floating through space.

24

❤ CA

life for a life

i gave my life for you
and you spit in my face
i tried to save you
from living the same fate
but you turned on me
in the blink of an eye
i don't know you anymore
that hurts so deep inside
i'm sorry i failed
i'm sorry for your pain
i'm sorry i couldn't get through
if only—gods how i've wished—
someone would save me
like i tried to save you

♥ CA

serrated knife

i can't keep doing this
i'm tired of muscling through it
if i just pull the rope a little tighter
i won't have to feel this
but i'm scared
i know my purpose in this life
i know this won't achieve that goal
but why does it have to feel like
i'm constantly being stabbed
with a fucking serrated knife
my lungs won't work without air
but honestly, i don't even know how
to stop and take a breath
is there even any time left?

❤ CA

i'm sorry

i'm sorry, truly
i wish i could do more
but i'm just trying to stop from
bleeding out on my bathroom floor

❤ CA

don't speak

did you know razor blades cut that deep?
did you attach them to your teeth?
please stop, your voice is grating
i'm barely hanging on
i'm dangling at the brink
it's better for me
if you don't speak.

❤ CA

there is *never* enough time in the fucking day

❤ CA

❤ CA

dark side

i was never afraid of the dark.
i just couldn't handle the light.

on growing

♥ CA

you lift me up
you let me breathe
wow, the validation you give me.
you don't do it on purpose
you aren't trying to impress
just living fully with love in your chest.
you show me patience
you make me kind
i'll love you for every piece of time.

❤ CA

hello darkness, my old friend

it hurts to move forward when the thoughts come in and
won't stop. i'm told to act happy and bring a smile, but
that mask is suffocating. no matter how big i smile or
how engaged i seem, my mind is spinning. that constant
movement is exhausting, and i just want to sleep.

why is sleeping a bad thing? our bodies need sleep.
maybe i need just a bit more than the typical person.

why is acting on how you feel a terrible thing?
why do i have to act how others want to perceive me?
why can't i just be me?
is it such a bad thing to feel lost and sad?
why can't i show the world how life makes me feel?

i'm told there is something wrong with me.
depression.

carrying these feelings throughout life has been
debilitating.
constantly holding my tongue and doing what i'm told is
right?
deafening.

♥ CA

acting how society feels is best is one of the most
polarizing things i've done.

yet, that is what i was taught is correct. now, when i am
finally free to be me and live the life i feel inside, i don't
know who that is anymore. i've lost what makes me me.
instead, i've become what my family and society have
made me to be.

i've become the perfect child, the ideal human to live in
this society. never stay out late, lie, or break the rules.
never tried new things because why fix what isn't
broken? i never had experiences in culture and life
because mine was "always better," so why risk it.

this is what i was taught since birth. these are my
learned behaviors and limiting beliefs. i know that now,
after years of therapy. but how do i change them?

how do i make the tornado of thoughts in my head go
away? i follow the steps my therapist tells me will help.
but, whenever i try to decide, the limiting beliefs swirl
around and fight for me to choose them.
which is the right choice?

❤ CA

how i feel inside or how i was taught my whole life?
how do i know the difference?
will someone tell me?
please?

never being able to test yourself in life is confusing.
never taking risks in life gets you nowhere. i don't know
how to move forward. i don't know what risks to take
after all these years of staying on the predetermined
path set out for me. now, i'm free to be me, but i don't
know who that is anymore.

now, all i feel is darkness. all of my emotions blend. all i
want is the sleep i was never allowed in my youth. now
i'm stuck. but is this truly what i feel inside?

why don't we change our thinking?

some days are better than others.
some days my moods vary.
some days my emotions run high.
some days my ambition seems low.
but now I know that for me, that is the beauty of life.

♥ CA

each day is unique.
each day is a chance to change something in your life
that didn't go well yesterday.
each day, there is time to improve on what you enjoy.
each day is a day to live.

i believe feeling the emotions and ups and downs of
each day and embracing them is the only way to move
forward, even when it's difficult.

so, why don't we choose emotions over perception? it
doesn't matter how i make you feel if i live my most
authentic life. how *i* make *you* feel simply represents
how you live your life, and how does that affect me?
short answer: **it doesn't.**

instead of impressing the person next to us, we could try
impressing ourselves. instead of worrying about how
others perceive our actions, pay attention to how we see
ourselves.

take pride in your sadness and make strides to bring joy
back to your life when the time is right. we are meant to

❤ CA

feel our emotions; we are meant to decide to change that
feeling if we want, but not for the pleasure of another.

that is my path in life, to feel again.

to live in that feeling for as long as i want. to not worry
about how i make you feel because those aren't my
feelings their yours. to sleep all day if i think that is best
and not care what is said about me.

change is difficult, especially in this world we live in. but
i plan to embrace the changes i'm making in all its forms
to live my most authentic life. isn't that the point of life,
to make it *unique* and make it **yours**?

❤ CA

identity, you lonely bitch

i lost my identity when i was 22.
i had only ever done one thing in my life—even if that
wasn't my choice—and it was just over.

i didn't realize until i was 25 that i had lost my identity
much earlier.
i might have never had one to begin with.

i knew i was the older sibling, and that made me
responsible.
i knew that softball was my life.
i knew money was necessary and could make things
better.
i knew i was different, and not everyone would be a fan
if i showed that.
i knew blending in meant a quieter day.
i knew these things because it was what i was told.

is that my identity? what even is an identity? does it
matter?
in this society, your identity keeps you in line.
it keeps you in check.

❤ CA

is that a different kind of identity?
is how i identify myself different than others?
how do you even identify yourself?

if i had to try and identify me, myself, and i,
i'm not sure what would fit.

i am abrasive, maybe bold.
i am strong yet weak.
i fight for love hard.
i live to break the rules.
i know what is right and what is wrong.
i know how to love and to hate.
i know always to put myself first.
i know my worth.

if that is my identity,
then i can accept it.
identity means something different to us all.
i keep my worth in mind when
the doubts start to creep in.

❤ CA

black swan

sometimes, i feel sad
sometimes, i feel lonely
sometimes, the black just never stops flowing.
which way is up
which way is down
which way makes it crumble to the ground?
i don't know who i am
i don't know where i'm going
i don't know if i can hold back,
these emotions that keep growing.
they poke and they prod
they creep and they crawl
they make me feel like starting a brawl
listen to my heart
listen to my mind
listen to my words just this one time.
acceptance is hard
acceptance is new
acceptance is pain,
not something i wish for you.
i'll keep moving forward
i'll keep pushing on
i'll keep my armor black, just like a swan.

❤ CA

death to self-expression

all the times i wanted
but never took the chance
created a hole inside me
death to self-expression.

everyone wanted me to change
forcing me to confirm,
giving in to those demands,
hurts like hell.

inside, i'm breaking
just hoping to find
kind and understanding humans with
love for who i am inside.

masking is all i know,
never sure who deserves my soul.
on the outside
perfection, yet
quiet thoughts destroy my creativity.

❤ CA

regrets fill me.
sometimes it's too much,
taking a step back
ultimately saved me.

visions of my life come to me
where do i go from here?
x-rays show the hole slowly closing,
yes, i can express myself again.

zen.

m.e.n.n.

up, down, left, right.
fuck, my chest is tight.
seven, eight, nine, ten.
only a few more seconds, and it'll end.
yes, no, maybe so.
does it intoxicate you, watching my crimson flow?
north, south, east, west.
does anyone care to hear my last breath?
read, write, listen, speak.
i refuse to be weak.
morning, evening, noon, night.
i'll be my own light.

♥ CA

it was gloomy today

it's gloomy today
so i got the urge
to express myself with these words.
the sun isn't yet up,
it's blocked from view
as grey opal clouds spread on through.
the blue sky that i love to watch,
it might not be your favorite
but to me
it calms the chaotic energy inside me.
the blues and whites turn to grey and black
like a rainbow of darkness, showing the path.
the path of change
the path of self-destruction
the path avoided by most
it might be hard but at least it's rewarding.
rewarding for me, not for you.
i promise this is me putting myself first
your words, your hate, your expectations
can take a hike.
i know what's best for me
this is MY LiFE.
if i want a haunted house to call home,
i'd be moving tomorrow.

♥ CA

if i wanted to grow under a gloomy, wet sky
i'd be living up north with some vampires by sundown.
just because it's dark, doesn't make it wrong.
if my shade of life is darker than yours,
you could be thanking me
for taking on the struggles you got to avoid.
but just because i am dark and you are light
doesn't mean we aren't alike.
we see the world on different sides of the same coin.
some would call that fate.
i'd call it purposeful.
but all i know right now is
it was gloomy out today,
and clearly, i needed to expel these words.

♥ CA

lucid dreams

i close my eyes and see things
sometimes they're too bright
i see the inside of me
thoughts
wishes
fears
doubts
they always circle about
does this mean that?
should i give in this time?
or do i let sleep take me instead?
i'll be here tomorrow night
falling into the rabbit hole
again and again.

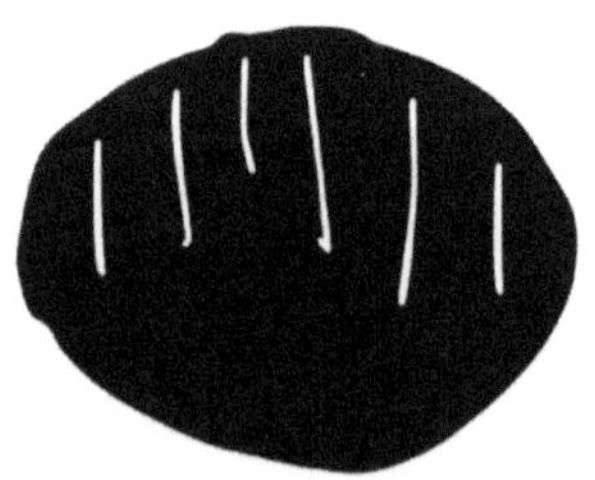

♥ CA

purge

desperation
 stress
  isolation
   anxiety
    depression
     stress
      overwhelm

whyyyyyy
do you act this way?

disconnected
 disturbed
  unchained

is there really no other way?

when my head's filled with thoughts
both intelligent and intrusive
mixing together, becoming one
my mouth doesn't know what to say

♥ CA

happiness
 joy
  excitement
  play

hopefully we'll get there one day,
but maybe not this day
for today, we purge it all away.

purge
purge
purge
purge purge
purge
purge
purge
purge purge

♥ CA

i have ptsd, karen, it's real

how do you stop it?

the video reel of trauma
from running on a loop

will it always be like this?

it hurts less each day
but i don't need a reminder

i was there
the trauma is mine
buried in the recesses
of my frazzled mind
the feelings might fade
but the visuals stay

maybe one day
at a certain time
the credits will finally run
that day is not today
but i have hope i'll find
the ending...someday

49

❤ CA

i can see you
can you not see me?
is it so hard to try
and hear my ideas when i speak?
does my voice grate on your ears,
like a chalkboard in class?
because i am so sick of falling flat on my ass.
falling on deaf ears might just be a saying
but that's what it feels like when i explain things.
i know i talk fast
i know i forget some words
but fuck me, can't you grade on a curve?
some of us can't understand or think
the same way as you
but that doesn't make me wrong
or not even worth listening to.
i need you to *try* to see me
like i *try* to see you
it won't always be roses and daisies
but fuck, is that so hard to do?

❤ CA

hard

this life is hard
like hollow bones
riddled with decay
but still they cling

the years of sickness
you spent fighting
finally, seeping through the decades of
old cracks that never healed fully.
is the fight worth it anymore?

soft

the end is soft
earth-scented pillows catch your head
colors will bloom
come springtime and fall

seeds will sow from your essence
it sounds so *easy* compared
to this torture

maybe life should be hard
even though i loathe that word

♥ CA

it **shouldn't** exist
because i CAN or COULD
do whatever i please

maybe the hardest decision in this life
is knowing when to stop
the finality of one
the beginning of another

no matter
in this life or next
hard times WILL come
so do the hard shit
because
you might not get to
in the next one

the only guarantee in life is right now
the only guarantee in death
is a soft landing.
choose hard or soft
it doesn't matter
you'll get both

❤ CA

i think the idea
is to live until you won't.

❤ CA

my head hits the wall with a crack
the pain is deafening, but i hear every word
every slur
every curse
every sin from your lips
i don't cower
no matter how violently i shake inside
i stand my ground
i talk back
because no one will ever treat me like that
this show runs on repeat
i'm used to the scars
but you will never beat me
i'm written in the stars
you'll never be worthy of me
and that makes you seethe
but i know my worth, i can take your reign
bitch i'm priceless,
move your broke ass away from me

❤ CA

clean dishes

please clean the dishes
i don't want to fight
i know my way of doing this
might not be right.
i know my trauma created a monster
but has common courtesy died out?
i swear it's been so long, something is starting to sprout.
i can only use a few items at a time,
then they *must* be cleaned
sorry but it's called OCD.
it doesn't have to be immediate
but fuck please make it clean.
i'll rein in my feelings
give you some time
i just can't hear another gastlit excuse
"i'll do it another time, it's fine"
i'm begging you now
its called give and take
hello, a relationship is **two-way**.
otherwise, what's the point?
i might as well start digging my own grave.

♥ CA

i swear i won't bite

please,
give me your feedback
tell what you think
tell me how you would've done it better than me
tell me how you would have gone left when i went right
tell me, i swear i won't bite.

i thrive in ebony, your sparkles are gilded
so how am i supposed to hear this?
understand? immediately change course?
ever thought there are more ways than yours?
my process is mine, but you say it's erratic
i'm telling you there's no way that hat fits.

let's try this again, stick a fork in this spaghetti,
i bet you cut it up with that butter knife.
you've really never thought of trying a little twist?
the result is a fucking *chef's kiss!*
but don't take it from me, try it yourself
it's not my job to help you find the way out.

❤ CA

you've never allowed me to do me, everyday it's you
and now you want to give me your feedback
after i've finally cut you loose?
i have manners so i'll listen, give you a shot
but my pot is full of ravens now
don't panic when your dreams for me start to **rot**.

♥ CA

you think you're so cool, don't you?
aesthetic hair
expensive clothes
are those red soles on your shoes?
i can't tell you how far from cool
that makes you
unless you mean the other kind of cool
the frigid kind, like opening the freezer door?
like how you iced me, my dreams, my aspirations,
put my life in a block of ice too?
that's the only kind of cool i see in you

❤ CA

co-dependency

i have to save myself
i can't keep putting it on you
it's just really hard to see anything
but the color blue
copying means flattery
please don't be mad
i'm just trying to find the next step
if anything, be glad
i won't be solely your responsibility
it won't all be on you
i'm taking my power back
and giving it my all
through and through

❤ CA

i'm trying this new thing
it's going well, actually
that's the honest truth
but i know that doesn't mean much to you
i'm writing my feelings down
all of them
until my fingers fall off
it's what i *have* to do
i can't find another way to let go
of all the bullshit you put me through

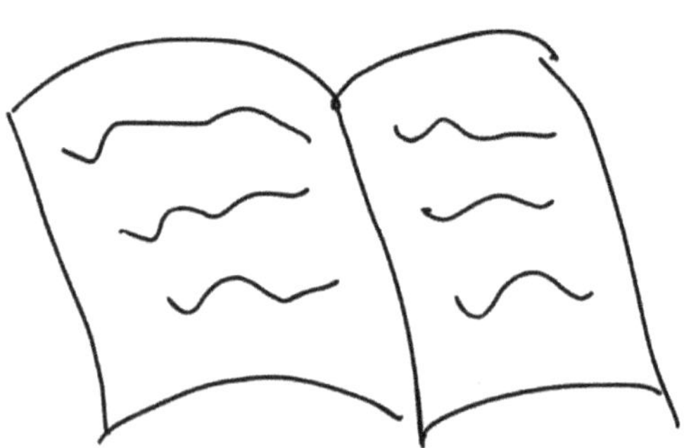

♥ CA

floating islands

good call
good catch
you beautiful brain of mine
i knew you didn't atrophy
after all this time
sometimes your slow
sometimes your speed is lightning
i finally understand how to use you
properly
little islands floating in my head
i can control them all
or let them peel off
dead
check back tomorrow
to see which way they fall

♥ CA

do tattoos hurt?
of course they fucking hurt
there's a needle in my thigh
but the pain only lasts a second
then the numbness arrives

go ahead, roll your eyes
but all you need is a distraction
then the endorphins start to flood in
that pain becomes nonexistent
and the happy chemicals kick in

for someone like me who can't regulate
getting tattooed is like eating
a **massive** slice of cake
i want that feeling to spread
over and over again

feel the rush in my veins on a loop
yes, tattoos are addictive, that's so true
but you have to get past the pain
be mentally tough
you can't just muscle through

❤ CA

so yes tattoos hurt,
but more like pulling a tooth
the best part is waking up
to the treat under your pillow
a nice little dopamine hit

except with tattoos,
you get that treat for life
and every time you look in a mirror
you get another hit
it's fucking bliss

❤ CA

roses are blue
violets are black
there's so much left for you in this life
don't give up just yet
you're sadness is your superpower
take it in stride
don't let ANYONE tell you
how you're feeling inside
sometimes laughter is sad
and pleasure brings tears to your eyes
the point is you are **you**, not them
no longer do they control
the thoughts in your mind
i implore you to release the scream
buried deep down inside
see what bubbles to the surface
i bet it'll leave you surprised
love yourself as you are, darling
you look beautiful in blue.

♥ CA

serendipity only occurs when you take a chance
a chance at love
a chance at success
you have to feel it in your chest
so take a step off the worn-down path
make your best guess
serendipity will find you
when you *decide* you're ready for that next step

❤ CA

on loving

♥ CA

ecstasy

drink me
from the nectar
on my tongue
taste my essence
as you swallow
my pain
my fear
my soul
devour me whole.

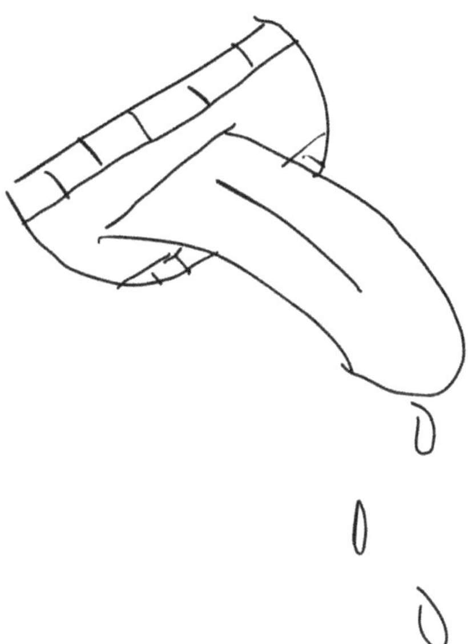

❤ CA

present yourself young sire

surrender your sword
to my womb
present your sapphire staff
let it gleam and glisten in the light
then press it deep inside
like glow in the dark, light me up inside
young sire please, i cannot wait any longer

my lady
the time and the place
i must protest
you deserve more than a quick flight
even though i can
take you to your highest height
now is a drastic point in time
i want to give you roses, and diamonds, all the pinks
your presence is soothing—just let me take one drink.
one taste of those lips could last a lifetime.

one drink always turns into another
one taste just makes you want more
why wait when you know how this path ends
my presence soothes you?
your skin is a balm

❤ CA

if i could put it on and wear it, oh darling,
i'd be the pick of the ball,
everyone would want a piece.
but...i don't like sharing
so i say finish me now
let the world see how your skin makes me crawl
...*please?*

you drive a *hard* bargain
dearest mine
i will cave to you this one
and only time.
cross your feet
look at me
open wide, oh how those pearly whites shine
i'll love you forever
with baby blue Forget-me-nots
so take a deep breath, sink to those knees
you know how much i *devour* hearing you
say please.

❤ CA

pink flower

flowers are my favorite
lush, juicy, always pink
not the biggest fan of heat
they wilt and die
but their roots go deep
through the ashes they rise
a phoenix emerging
watch her fly

no two smells the same
it's a dangerous game to play
luring you in for a quick bite
even though it's not right
but loyalty bleeds from your eyes
you'd never stray
when i can satisfy
my heat is your favorite
honeydew on your tongue
taste me *lover* until the sun comes

❤ CA

release me

more
i need more
want to taste your breath
imprint you on my skin
tattoo you on my lungs
more
i want more
want to feel you inside
release me from my shackles
make me feel alive

❤ CA

act natural...natural, natural, natural.

don't show too much
you'll lose him

don't let him see those scars
he'll find you disgusting

don't be unique
pull that mask on tighter

act natural!
natural...right, i can do that.

i'll curl my hair and put on a pretty dress
keep my mouth shut until i need a breath
be the woman i've been told to be
that works for you, right?
even if it's not really me?

i don't know how else to keep your love with me.

❤ CA

porn

sitting in the adjacent room
minding my peace silently
wishing that you'd play with me
but your mind is elsewhere
definitely not on me
you'd rather watch
fake tits
fake hair
forced ecstasy
i knew there was something wrong with me
i knew this love wouldn't keep
too many sins
too many red flags
too unlovable it seems
now i know you actually needed more from *me*
the words never crossed your lips
but when i mention it that's all i can see
written across your face
your eyes filled with grief
maybe next time,
try and talk to me?

❤ CA

night sweats

in the heat of the night,
is it you or me?
sweating through the sheets
tossing and turning from anxiety.

our bodies millimeters apart
but our minds live in a different state
lightyears between.

i want you, but i'm scared to lay bare
i want you to want me,
but my insecurities control me
could i kiss you, just there?

move a little left
then go right
that's it baby
just this time

how do people sleep in this heat every night?

❤ CA

do you love me? i ask for the hundredth time.
no matter the answer, my insecurities still thrive.
i pick up the rose and start again,
hopeful that i can figure out the end.
because i love you even it you love me not.
you say the petals fall in my favor, but i don't trust that.
because those white lies still freely flow,
from me to you and back again.
what happens when the rose is bare at the end?
i'll find a way to be worthy of your love.
even if i have to glue the petals back on the bulb.

❤ CA

eyes

them eyes look at me
and i see the whole world in one blink.
blues and greens, the color purple
how deep does your well go?
i'll swim even when
all you see is murky green
fishing for stars, it's easy
those gilded pools are abundant.
you've seen the darkest trenches
as they've ripped through me
i appreciate you wholly
for seeing the silver streaked whirlpools within me.

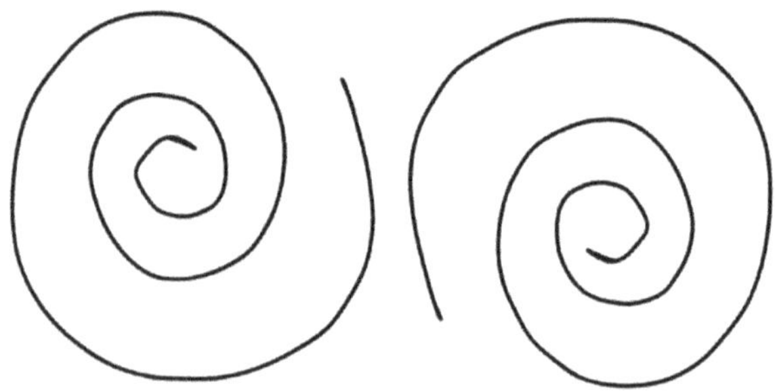

76

❤ CA

stray cat

when my emerald eyes bleed black, i turn left
towards the light i dash, you cannot see that
love is fickle, yours feels like petty theft
just a little mouse caught by a stray cat

i try to conform, but my hands are stained,
black is all i see.
please just go away
your light glows so bright tell me, is it feigned?
i see ravens when you see doves streaked gray

our love is something out of fiction, babe
two opposites attract, is this real life?
you showed me how to finally escape
i still cannot believe that i'm your wife

lover boy, you taught this heart to grow
without you here, there'd be no me to know

❤ CA

this minute

everything is different now.
yesterday was there, while today is here.
leaves crunch beneath my cold toes
as i walk this forest path.
the wetness of the sky matches
how you make me feel inside.
i brush my palms against the rough bark
of our tallest redwood tree.
it reminds me of how it feels when you touch me.
callused hands from a long day's work, roam my skin
looking for a perch.
do the blue birds know your intent?
can they hear your siren song playing in my head?
legs trembling, my back hits the ground
as i watch the sky come alive.
hours pass, now streams of white cotton
cover me head to toe.
the twinkle from the lights we hung above
exposes my glow.
i'd let you paint me in your essence forever.
the blues, reds, greens—all the colors of the wind.
they breathe life into my monochrome world.
are we finishing here? on this forest path?
we're hidden from the world, but i feel the eyes peeping.

❤ CA

that extra push always sends me over, and your waiting.
my voice, finally released from the golden shackles
i find so hard to break,
scattering the birds above; can you feel their fate?
or is it only me you can read
like a book you wrote yourself?
put me in your pocket and take me home.
place me back on the shelf until you're ready for more.
i'll bask in your light until the bulb breaks,
because without you,
my life feels like the forest in the dead of winter.
black, frigid, lifeless.
so for this minute, will you take my hand?
let me breathe life into you as you do for me.
and please, love, please don't ever leave this forest
without me.

❤ CA

burned heart

black
barren
loss of life

the organ in my chest put up a good fight
it fought and clawed until it bled no more
burned to a crisp.

but wait, what's that little door?

how did you find that key?
i swear it's invisible to me,
you unlocked the chains i thought would last forever
do you take your love, extra crispy?

this heart's been burned many a times,
i smothered the fire until it only simmered
but you're telling me it tastes divine?

my heart burns for you
i can't put it out—nor would i even try
do you want some fire proof gloves?
will that help?
will that keep you by my side?

❤ CA

the way you explore
savoring my taste
fuck, it puts me in a state

state of delusion because
i swear this can't be right
i didn't even have to put up a fight.

you give and you give
the seasoning is excellent
that charcoal on your tongue
oooh—makes my head spin

thank you for not giving up
on this burned heart.

❤ CA

taste this butter

satisfied.
accepted.
euphoric.
happy.

show me the bread and pass the butter;
i always want to feel this way.

it might be a pile of flour, water, and salt,
but i was always satisfied.
the flour filled my stomach when nothing stayed down.
the water nourished my body
since i couldn't do it myself.
the salt gave me that taste of freedom i craved.

it could've been a piece or even a loaf, but i felt accepted.
the judgment didn't follow my choice to indulge...which
was different, yet liberating.
the amount didn't matter
i could take as much fuel as i needed.
the idea of eating didn't feel so arduous.

it didn't matter what toppings came with;
having a choice was euphoric.

❤ CA

the butter was always smooth as silk,
tattooing a smile on my face.
the mixture of oils transports you
to a world of pure bliss.
the scents and sounds i savored, absolutely intoxicating.

it was my favorite snack because it was the only food
that made me happy.
the bread made me glow.
the butter brought me joy.
the belief in myself rose with each delectable bite.

bread and butter for snack time: *helped me feel alive.*

happy.
euphoric.
accepted.
satisfied.

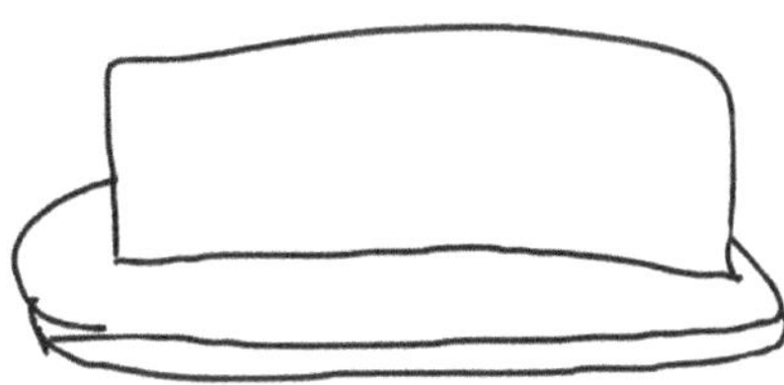

♥ CA

frosted pain

black, darkness
creak, crack
white, starkness
creak, cracked
frosty, harshness
snap, crack
lush, coolness
woosh, snapped
blue, heartless
creak, crack
pale, colorless
creak, cracked

the ice falls down my window in a drop of color.
black fades to white as white turns to blue
as blue becomes pale.
the glistening frost snaps and cracks
as it melts on the sill.
watching the fall leaves turn to dead trees
as the winter sleep sweeps in,
is my ideal way to pass the time.

♥ CA

indulging in you—for free, mind you—until the
darkness fades,
definitely helps the clock hands
tick, tick, away.
creak, crack, my frost is black.

❤ CA

firsts

so many have been with you, all have been unique.
there's one i'm waiting for with bated breath,
it's making me count sheep.
my womb weeps at the thought
of our first time.
cream & cherries
cherries & cream
the order doesn't matter to me.
the when
the where
the why
i just can't take the lie.
i want to feel swollen with golden rain.
the first step and a high five.
i want to absorb the unconditional love
and project it times five.
i want the pain and confusion
because the outcome is worth it.
i want to watch their growth,
see the strength of their back.
how much longer must i wait for that?
first ten years, plus two more.
i said it was okay but now...
now i think i need more.

❤ CA

eternal flame

let me taste your fire
so fucking sweet
i could live off you for eternity
tell me your mine
say you'll take my name
i'll love you always and forever
never doubt our eternal flame

❤ CA

river god

it's crazy to think how happy
i thought i was
before you showed me differently
the unconditional love i didn't know i needed
is what you freely give me
i love you today, tomorrow, and forever
little boy
i hope you feel my love for you always
times infinity

❤ CA

unwritten

sometimes loving someone
means leaving them alone
you have their heart
you are their home
distance makes the heart grow fonder
as the old saying goes
and right now i love you
but please
let me debrief on my own

❤ CA

communication is key
you can't talk to me
you can love me
period.

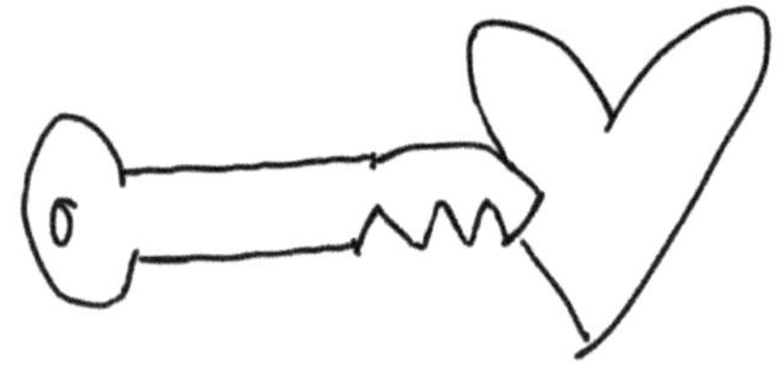

❤ CA

i love it when you ask me
you want to hear me speak
i love it when i can ramble
thoughts just pouring out of me
i'm not thinking you'll keep up
or even understand
then you ask me another question
like you're fully invested
i love it when you hear me
you let me be free
thank you for taking a chance on me

❤ CA

moonlit serenade

kiss me
under the moonlight
let the stars witness
they can look but not touch
push me up against the tallest tree
let the leaves rain down in glee
i love you more each day
i hope this feeling never fades

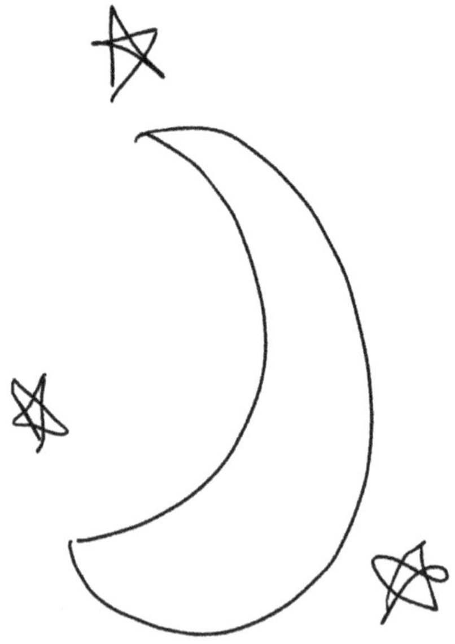

♥ CA

beautiful mind

the thing i love most
is how you make me feel
not the butterflies
not the ecstasy
but fuck it's so real
the way you care
the way you listen
how you let me be me
the thing i love the most
is your beautiful mind
and how it sees me

93

♥ CA

on healing

♥ CA

authenticate me.

2fa
sms
passkey
is that what authenticate means?
numbers and words thrown together
made to confuse
sounds like a lot of hoops to jump through
just to access the me in my mind
but that's safer, right?
place a boundary
put up a fight
if you really want me, show me your light
authenticate me, but you only get three tries
or i'll stick you in a cell, a prisoner you'd be
i promise you it no longer bothers little ole me.

♥ CA

this is hard
writing is hard
expressing myself is hard
being **me** is hard
i feel like an imposter daily
but i'm hopeful these words will save me

❤ CA

little mouse

sometimes
it is in the
silence
where we are the
loudest.

❤ CA

goodbye little ants

it crawls and creeps
it pokes and prods
it lives within
it digs deep down
it's darkness envelopes
it tries to control
but i won't let it
not today
not anymore.

❤ CA

world's heaviest backpack

it is always with me.
i carry it on my back.
i project it to the world.
but i am none the wiser.

i continue my scratching and stimming until someone
asks, "are you okay?" then, thinking back to what i had
been doing, i didn't even realize i looked unwell. so i
reply, "yeah, i'm fine." not wanting my worries to further
burden those around me.

anxiety is me, and i am anxiety. i have never known any
difference.

living with anxiety is like living with a separate
consciousness that tells you all your worries at once. it's
goal is to be overwhelming, because if it isn't, we won't
listen. so no matter how i'm feeling—happy, sad, or
excited—that consciousness inside is constantly
worrying about something.

it always tells me the negative outcomes of my desires,
so i am stagnating.

♥ CA

it always tells me the world's poor perception, so i'm overly cautious.

it always tells me to stay safe at all costs, so i'm isolated.

nowadays, anxiety is thrown around daily. the phrase "i have anxiety" is as common as saying, "i love you." and just like that three-word idiom, most don't truly understand the meaning. if i say, "i have anxiety," most people will respond with, "oh, okay, me too. it's been a tough week."

is that *really* anxiety? do you feel what i'm feeling?

do you sit on your couch trying to watch TV, attempting to relax and unwind, and suddenly get a burst of adrenaline? does it make your heart feel like it will beat out of your chest? like your breath is running away with no chance to catch it?
it's not from the wholesome cooking show, you're watching. it's from your other consciousness worrying about something completely unrelated. the adrenaline and thoughts take over your mind, and you **cannot** concentrate on anything. you suddenly begin to itch all

❤ CA

over your body, prepared to give yourself more scars just
to make it stop. this is what i mean when i say, "i have
anxiety."

silent panic.
squirming.
itching.
hiding.
deafening.

maybe you've experienced a silent panic attack. the
silence is because you are in public and don't want to
worry others with your problems. but the sound inside
your head is *deafening*.

maybe it was triggered by the number of people in your
social environment. *(this has happened to me)*
maybe it was triggered by an overheard conversation
that you now cannot unhear. *(this has happened to me)*
maybe it was triggered by a thought that your other
consciousness was worrying about, and now you are too.
(this has most definitely happened to me)

❤ CA

the first thing i do is to try and find some comfort.
maybe i cross my arms to protect myself from others if i
feel pressured in a social environment. sometimes i hold
my own hand. the pressure and reassurance you can give
yourself just by holding your hand is mesmerizing.

it makes me feel safe, in control, and accepting of my
feelings. because there is nothing wrong or negative
about these feelings, they are just *uncomfortable*.

honestly, one could argue that the only way to move
forward is to constantly feel uncomfortable.

where's that data?

everyone has different anxieties, worries, feelings,
emotions, etc. none are wrong, maybe just not helpful.
for example, my therapist constantly tells me to find
data for my thoughts and feelings. if i can't find tangible
evidence that what i'm thinking or feeling is correct, i
push it away because it's not helpful.

it's not helpful to feel constantly on edge.

❤ CA

it's not helpful to feel pressured when making any
movement.
it's not helpful to worry about every minute detail in
your daily life.
it's not necessary to control it all. but **that is anxiety.**

that is the overarching message my therapist tells me
and what i tell myself when i have these feelings of
anxiety. of course, it isn't always straightforward, and
sometimes i need more. but this is always my first step:
where's the data?

now breathe.

it took me about 24 years to really look at and
understand my anxiety. i had been living with it for so
long i never realized what it was. i never connected the
dots to my feelings, emotions, and reactions. but, once i
started therapy, we realized what was going on, and
together we have been able to navigate my mind so i can
live my life.

❤ CA

i like to think of when i started going to therapy as the first time i stopped to take a breath. it was the first time i could work on myself and talk to someone who was truly there for me and only me. now, of course, it's been years since i started seeing her, and my anxiety is still present. but it is now **manageable**. something i never thought possible. being able to control my life, feelings, and emotions fully has opened up a world of possibilities. taking a breath and changing what i'm thinking is like magic. i thoroughly recommend you try it.

my anxiety might be the itch i can't scratch, but i'm not itchy today.
i can send that feeling away if **i choose**.
i can embrace it if **i choose**.
i can change it if **i choose**.
but only if **i choose**.

❤ CA

this one's for you
little Annie Lou
your voice was strong
but the sea ripped it away
leaving you to drown
i hope this speaks to you
i hope your soul can live free and
finally heal

♥ CA

in, out.
breathe.
up, down.
breathe.
front, back.
breathe.
fast, slow.
breathe.
high, low.
breathe.

there are so many versions of breath
so many different melodies.
there are various feelings attached.
they create a song.
a song of sorrow or hurt,
maybe a happy one.
sometimes loud, sometimes soft
but always easy to catch on.
breath can bring light to your eyes
or drag you to darkness.
it can lift you higher
or bring you down to kiss the ground.
breath is yours to own,

❤ CA

rarely challenged by another.
take your breath in stride
and open a world of endless desires.

breath is stirring
breath is strong
breath is luring
breath is long
breath is blurring
breath is as a birdsong.

how do you breathe?

do you relish in each person's uniqueness and try to
make it your own? or do you follow the flow of those
around you and breathe another's song?

i invite you to try the breathing technique that resonates
with you the most. understanding how the breath moves
through the body and affects you will bring new life to
your every second.

that is what breath does: *it brings us a few more seconds of
life each time we inhale.*

❤ CA

humans inhale between 12 and 20 times each minute. so why not try to make it your own? why not pay attention to how you breathe and what you experience with every inhale?

everyone is unique, everyone breathes differently. understanding your distinct way of breathing and how it influences your actions will open your eyes to a different way of living.

you can create a song entirely your own if you pay attention to those minute changes that each breath makes you feel.

breathe.
high, low.
breathe.
fast, slow.
breathe.
front, back.
breathe.
up, down.
breathe.
in, out.

♥ CA

therapy goddess

they say she's a goddess
cloaked in white light
but really her therapy is going alright
she found someone for her who listens and digests
instead of spewing venom back at her chest
she's learned to hold things close
not give everyone a chance
because honestly, they don't deserve it
and she just wants to land,
softly on her feet this one fucking time
she pleads and begs
so to therapy she takes herself
to understand the fuckery in her head

❤ CA

I AM

anger
disgust
frustration
why do you make me feel this way?
hurt
disrespect
confusion
not once have you asked if i'm okay.

i know feelings are feelings
and i don't have to feel this way
i've given you power over me
it stops today.

i am smart
i am kind
i am strong,
especially when i feel this way.
this page is stained with tears
i can't hold in another day
but not for you, for me
these feelings you caused
leak out of me in streams
i'm not sure how to stop.

♥ CA

but tomorrow is a new day
i PROMISE all you'll feel is rueful.
because i'm walking away,
i know longer need your approval.

❤ CA

color theory

gilded cage, so no one asks.
scarlet in color means pain, don't show that.
green little soul finally standing tall,
shhh spinebreakers live down the hall.
fuchsia dreams come at a cost,
are you ready for that cross?
raven nights lead to gloomy days,
wow you've become so brave.

♥ CA

after sundown
i just want to lie down
it's hard to find my way down
but when i let this weight down
i'll be headed straight down
so go ahead, i'll let my hair down
just know, we don't have to stay down
but on this trip, let's keep our heads down
the sunset sugar will help the medicine go down.

❤ CA

are you ready yet?

is that question for me or you?
am i ready yet?
what's it to you?
i'll be ready when i decide,
"not a minute earlier!" i cry
it could be today or tomorrow, maybe two weeks' time
but the choice is *mine*—not yours
that's a hill i'd die for.
"you'll never be ready, you just have to do it."
HA. i promise i don't have to do shit
we both bleed the same shade of red
but that doesn't mean you can see inside my head
if you're ready, that's great for you
but that doesn't mean i have to be ready too
i've come to learn "ready" is a state a mind
what's so beautiful about that, you ask?
there's no designated length of time
that i *have* to decide to do anything in this life
you'll know when i'm ready, or maybe you won't
i severed the umbilical cord wrapped around my throat

❤ CA

titanium skin

your claws used to be embedded in my skin
you liked me that way, obedient and thin
you never stopped to think on what you were creating
you never cared to ask how badly i was breaking
you burned
you plucked
you ripped
you sheared
you made me terrified of every mirror
you know it now, but i lived it then
you could have just tried being my friend
your blood red claws left hundreds of tattoos
you hurt me bad, but made me stronger too
my skin is titanium now after what i endured
try all you want now
you won't even leave a bruise

❤ CA

temple of aphrodite

don't eat too much you'll get fat
don't wear that it's too tight,
no one likes that
be healthy
be strong
go workout
go be seen
but don't be too much, it scary.

you're sooo skinny, eat more!
you look sick, what's wrong with you?
do you even have muscle on you?
those baggy clothes don't fit, get new ones
your older now, act your age
go fix your hair, you look deranged

my body is a temple, they said
but it can never measure up
i ate what you wanted, wore expensive clothes
but there's still something wrong
it must be me—i'm just a dumb whore

❤ CA

well you know what fuck you,
i'm done listening to your vile
i'll be healthy, happy, alive
but for ME not you
i'll paint my closet black
darkness has always been my home
now watch, keep your eyes peeled
as Aphrodite worships ME
while i'm sitting on her throne.

♥ CA

guns and roses

black nails
lace bra
tattoos
baggy tees
gauges—eep
fast talking
misdirection
mental case
that's how you see me

artistic soul
compassion
emotions on my sleeve
passion
expression
sensuality
brave heart
creativity
that's the real me

❤ CA

try walking through the looking glass
and you'll see *me*
singing guns n' roses
with a cheshire cat
i'm finally free to be
irrevocably in love
with me.

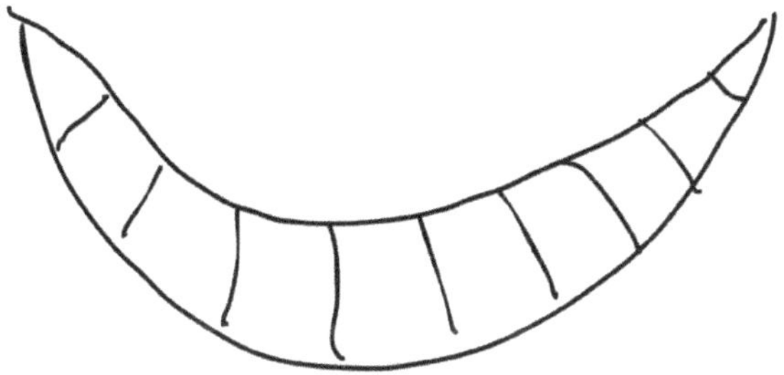

❤ CA

exfoliate the demons

i scraped my skin until it bled
pulled my hair out of my head
stopped eating until my skin pulled tight
bleached my teeth pearly white
but that horcrux wasn't dead
it survived *deep* inside my instead
my bones chipped, painted black
no matter how hard i scrubbed
i wasn't exorcising that

it took awhile, but i started to breathe again
realized the demon was controlling my zen
you know, the one you put inside my mind
and fucking hell, did it take a long time
i exfoliated that bitch until i cried.
and now my hands are no longer tied
to your life, your goals, your way of thinking
damn, never thought i could actually be me
but look at me now, just smiling sweetly.

♥ CA

october wishes

october gets a bad wrap
it's by far my favorite month of the year
probably because i've been treated so similarly
told i'm dark because of my choice of clothes
told i'm scary because i know my worth
told i'm silly because i let my inner child live her life
told i'm cold because i don't let the demons win
but october has always understood me
always given me a safe place to land
all my wishes have been granted
standing under an october harvest moon
with a midnight colored Raven upon my hand

❤ CA

growing older

growing older means putting yourself first
that's why i'm here right now
not for you, but for me
i'm glad my presence can calm you
but let's be honest, shall we
you took my life away
ripped my heart straight out of my chest
but growing older means
i can still wish you the best
it doesn't mean it changes things
it doesn't mean i accept your sorrow
it means i'm growing older
and i know what's important to me

❤ CA

good job buddy

patting myself on the back
for accepting my faults
learning from my mistakes
and taking the path less traveled
to become the human
i've always meant to be today

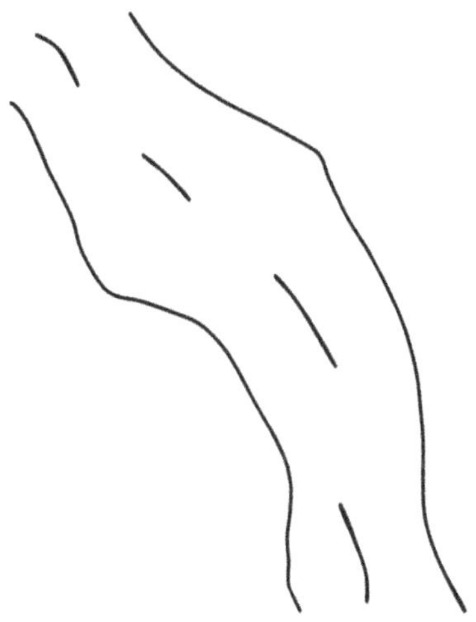

❤ CA

a little pain feels good sometimes

healing is weird.
you live your whole life a certain way
then one day
poof
everything changes
you don't talk to the same people
you don't dress the same way
your mind and body are on
a completely different path
and that's okay
you've been trekking the uphill battle
for far too long
you deserve the rest
and for the right people to cheer you on

that doesn't mean it's easy
change is fucking hard
it's heartbreaking
devastating
feels like losing an arm
but it's not forever
moving forward is the important part
as long as you stay true to you
and live with love in your heart

❤ CA

head trip

being neurodivergent in a neurotypical world
fuck, that's a trip
even when you are doing your best
you never seem to fit
i propose a new way of thinking
everyone's unique
everyone thinks differently
there's no need to put a box around us
the best part of coloring books
is coloring outside the lines
and creating freely
if we all tried to color outside the box
just a little bit
this world would flip on its head
that's my kind of head trip

♥ CA

rainbow melodies

hey annie lou,
how ya doing?
can you hear the music yet?
the path you wanted to take
is finally open, and you're free
let's leave a beautiful melody in our wake
cheers to the days that come
i honestly cannot wait,
to experience the music we create.

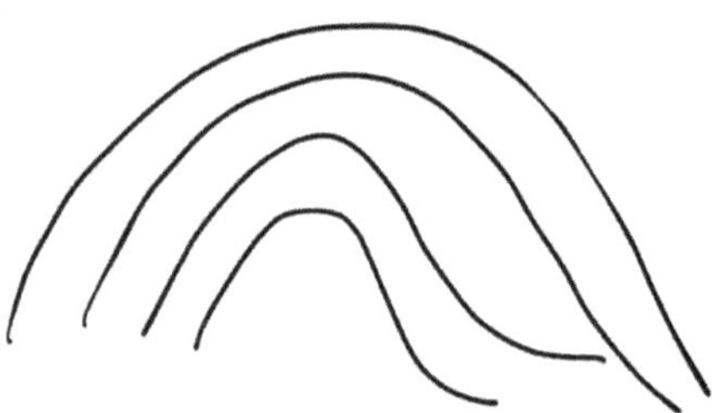

❤ CA

acknowledgements

thank you to everyone who has ever given me hope that this was possible. writing and publishing a book is hard. something i never thought i'd accomplish, even though it's been my dream since a young child. so thank you to those who believed in me despite the hard times. thank you to those who continue to support me in everything i bring to this life. your love means the world to me. lastly, thank you to my husband. my partner. my muse. the one constant in my rollercoaster of a life. i love you forever lover boy. thank you for being my light.

❤ CA

about the author

Courtney Ann writes love letters to the darkness and light. her debut collection, *lover boy: letters to my lover,* is a four-part journey through the landscapes of anxiety, depression, love, and ultimately, choosing yourself. she believes in feeling all your emotions, sleeping when you need to, and that anxiety might just be her emotional support demon. sometimes the hardest person to write a love letter to is yourself—but those are the most important ones to send. this is her first book, but not her last confession. you can find more of her work via her website courtneyannauthor.com.

♥ CA

♥ CA

yes means yes, right?

so you know how
yes means no,
but then also yes.
and if you say it
this way, "yes?"
it means maybe instead.
how am I supposed
to give consent,
when no doesn't always mean no
but sometimes yes?

♥ CA

www.ingramcontent.com/pod-product-compliance
Lightning Source LLC
Chambersburg PA
CBHW041332120726
48005CB00014B/2214